100 Study Tips That Work!

JOHN SMITH

a Smith Mathematics publication

Copyright 1999 John Smith

ISBN 0 9585724 29

No part of this publication may be reproduced, stored in a retrieval system, or transmitted in any form or by any means, electronic, mechanical, photocopying, recording or otherwise, without the prior permission of the publishers or copyright owners.

This book is available from any recognised bookseller or by contacting:

        Smith Mathematics Pty Ltd
        14 Kooloona Crescent
        West Pymble NSW 2073

        Telephone : (02) 9498 8883
        Fax :   (02) 9498 4118

Printed by Australian Print Group

100 Study Tips that Work!

TIP 1

Study Yourself!

To succeed at study, you must first study yourself!

Ask yourself:

What do I usually do as far as study is concerned?

Does it work?

Do I have bad study habits?

Have I changed my study habits as I have progressed through the school and the work has become harder?

As you learn more about yourself, you will come up with ideas to improve your study habits. Write them down and work on these ideas. If you are convinced that they might work, then try them. If they don't work then find some other way of studying. But whatever you do, think about it! Otherwise you will drift with no plan to help. Remember that your current habits have been with you a long time. If they are not working for you, then change them!!

Of course you may be 100% happy with your techniques and know with certainty that they are the best you could ever think of. Hence you don't need this book! Stop reading it now and go and write your own book.

100 Study Tips that Work!

TIP 2

List your strengths and weaknesses

Find out what you're good at and what always gives you trouble. Make a list of each. Show the list to your teacher and see what he/she thinks of your abilities.

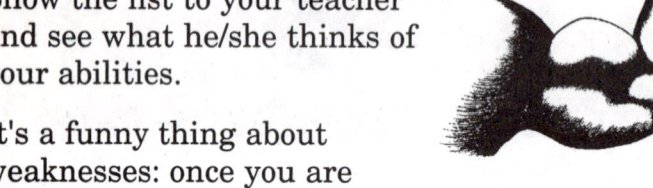

It's a funny thing about weaknesses: once you are aware of them, you can do something about them. Once you've done something about them, they become your strengths.

It makes you think: Those really smart people at school, the ones that always come up the top of any exam, are probably really stupid - but they've worked on fixing their weaknesses. So why shouldn't *you* be smart!?

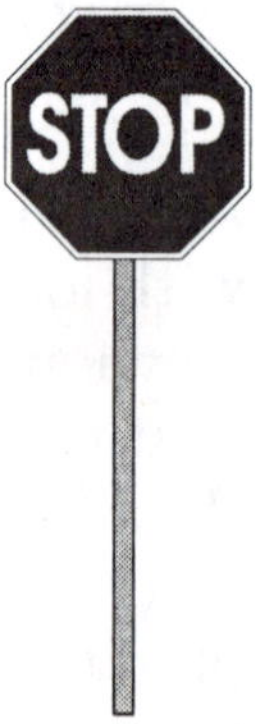

TIP 3

Know your limits

You must know your limits. How else can you exceed them? So, if you always get roughly 50% in English exams, find out from your teacher what your problem is. It may be lack

of knowledge, poor essay writing, lack of quotes or any number of other problems. Once you know what the problems are, you can do something about fixing them. But if you don't know them, how can you possibly get better?

TIP 4

Be Yourself!

Don't blindly adopt the study habits of someone else - unless you are convinced that they will work for you as well. The needs of someone else will almost certainly differ from your own, simply because they know different things than you do.

And your progress will usually be slow - very slow. For example, you've been told that reading as much as possible will help your marks. But reading one book is unlikely to raise your marks. Perhaps it will take years of reading before you see a difference between you and the person who doesn't read at all. But when you *do* see a difference - then, you'll *really* see a difference! Essays will flow from your pen. Ideas will come from thin air. The changes that you will have made to yourself will amaze you. And this is just recreational reading - not reading for study purposes!

Being yourself is all you need to be. Add the techniques from this book and you can grow into a person that other people wish to be.

100 Study Tips that Work!

TIP 5

Listen to suggestions from anyone

Having said that, listen to advice from any of your friends or family. Perhaps the secret to study success is as close as the person sitting alongside of you at school. Ideas from other people can suggest what you can do. But equally, they can help you avoid mistakes.

Listen to your family. Your parents sat for exams too!

Listen to your teachers. They may know more than you know!

And be sure you do <u>listen</u> to them. You don't have to <u>act</u> on anyone's advice, but it won't hurt you to listen.

Who knows: Perhaps .....

> *What is the difference between a deaf person and one who will not listen? The deaf person is seldom stupid.*
>
> *Anon*

TIP 6

Find out about your course!

Make sure of what the course entails. Seek your teachers' help in this. Otherwise you may waste valuable time in studying the wrong topics. Remember that there are two types of material to study:

    i)   The core material

    ii)   The support material

The core material is the stuff that you *must* know. In History, for example, you may need to know dates, causes of events and so on.

The support material is the stuff that makes the core material come to life. Perhaps there is a video on this topic, perhaps there are other books you could read, perhaps there is a documentary on TV.

It's not uncommon for a History student to have 10 or more books and several videos on support material, and only one book on the core.

If your teachers cannot help you find extra material, don't forget the library. Often libraries contain material that your teachers haven't come across.

When you are asking advice from teachers, make sure you ask about both core and support.

TIP 7

Fix your Attitude

The correct mental set is important. Think of your study time as a battle field on which are two warriors.

One warrior is **What You Know**.

The other is **What You Don't Know**.

Of course there is so much more that you don't know, that it's easy to get discouraged. But we all started out knowing nothing! And now look at us: We can cross roads, boil water and hundreds of other dangerous things. Conquering a subject may be difficult. But it can be done! And you are one of those who are going to do it!

TIP 8

Be Prepared for Temptations

Be mentally prepared. Your friend rings just as you are about to start studying. *"What about a game of tennis?"* *"Let's go to the movies"* You must be mentally tough enough to say No!! Explain to your friend that you are on a <u>Timetable</u> <u>to</u> <u>Success</u>! Ask for a raincheck. But be prepared before it happens. You are working on Long Term Goals not Short Term Pleasures!

This does not mean that you cut yourself off from friends or family. It just means that when you make a promise to yourself, you keep it.

And of course, you *should* have leisure time as part of your timetable. And if you can juggle your study time and your leisure time, then do so. If you have a 3 hour break timetabled for tomorrow, then use tomorrow's leisure time today. Go to the pictures. Have a game of tennis. But tomorrow, you must make up the time from today.

TIP 9

What about Panic??

If you are going to panic, panic early!! It is a great motivator and you can use it to speed up your preparation. However, it's useless to panic a day before your exams. If you have left it too late, you can always

ask a question

glance at a book

jot down a list of topics

right up until your exam. Some students claim to have asked a question of a friend on the way into the exam, and that question *has been on the paper!* You can be lucky - but ....

TIP 10

When should I start studying?

When should you start studying for the final exam?

Now!!

Try this:

Put this book down for 10 minutes and go to your desk and learn *one idea* for your next exam! In 10 minutes you should be able to:

i)   Learn the idea

ii)   Record it in your Night-Before-the-Exam Book - see Tip 32

iii)   Put it in your school diary, ready for revision - see Tip 40

TIP 11

But I can't get organised!

Join the club!! Unless you are a very rare person, you will have to *learn* to be organised. Like learning how to remember, this is something that students do!!

Think of this:

If the TV went on the blink, you'd have it fixed as soon as possible! You would look up the number of the repair business. You'd phone them to come and fix the TV - *now*! If they couldn't come at once, you'd find somebody who could. And once you had found someone who could fix the TV *right now*, you'd keep their name and number on the fridge door for future reference.

Now, that's being organised! And you can do that without thinking!

And that's what you should do with your study, your mistakes and things that you don't understand.

TIP 12

Essays take too much time

To run a race of 400m, you practise running 400m - not the high jump. To be able to write essays in, say, 20 minutes, practise writing essays in 20 minutes. Get someone to choose a topic for you, set the clock and go for it. Your improvement will amaze you! If no-one can think of a topic, open an encyclopedia and write an essay on the first picture you see. Part of the skill in writing essays is to be able to write on topics that you know little about. You never get essays in exams that are exactly what you want, so practise this way.

And the advice from <u>all</u> teachers of essay subjects is to read, read, read! The more books you consume, the better prepared you will be. These are not necessarily text books, just any book will do.

By reading, you exercise your imagination,

>you learn new words,

>you are exposed to new ideas

>and you enjoy yourself.

There is no course in the world that could teach all these. And, these are the very skills that will increase your essay writing abilities and hence, decrease the time you need to write one.

100 Study Tips that Work!

TIP 13

Find out about the exam

What topics will be tested?

What are the likely essays?

How many questions are there?

How many essays?

How many hours will the exam be?

What sort of exam is it? *Multiple choice?*

Open book?

Free response?

Do I need special instruments? Compass? calculator?

Will I need to draw diagrams?

Can I get past papers?

TIP 14

How do I prepare for essay exams?

If you know that there will be an essay on Augustus Caesar in the exam, you must do at least 2 things in preparation:

1   Learn the facts - and ensure that you remember them.

2   Practise writing essays on Augustus

But which essays? While you are learning the facts, try to make up essay topics.

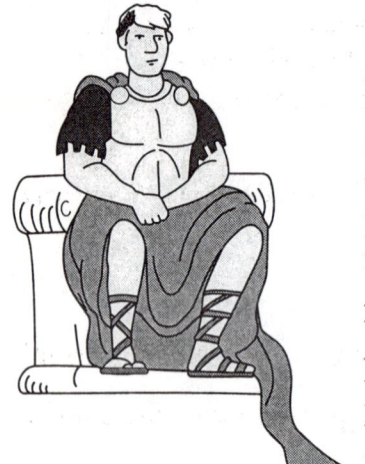

Perhaps you just learned how Augustus came to power. OK so write an essay on the question "Describe the means whereby Augustus came to power". Or, perhaps you've just read what happened during Augustus's time in power. Write an essay on "Describe how Augustus consolidated his power".

If you just learn the facts, you will have great difficulty in writing an essay for the first time in the exam. If you have practised writing essays, you will remember sentences and paragraphs that you can use, even if the topic in the exam is not one of those you have practised.

TIP 15

If I finish the exam early, what should I do?

Firstly, don't leave the exam room! Many exams allow you to leave as soon as you finish. But .....

A friend of mine tells a good story: He left his final Mathematics exam early. He'd finished as much as he could. He'd checked his work. He'd redone some questions he was doubtful about. He was satisfied he could do no more. So he handed in his paper and left the room. He'd walked 20m away from the exam room, when he remembered how to do Question 8 - one of the questions he'd left out! That question was worth 10 marks and he could have got full marks for it. He missed getting into University by 4 marks and had to repeat the year!!

And what should *you* do if you do finish early? Here are some ideas:

In mathematics or science exams:

i) Have you answered every part of every question?

ii) Have you got marks for questions you can't do? See Tip 94

iii) Check for mistakes

iv) Redo doubtful questions

v) See if your answer is reasonable

vi) Have you included the units: cm^2, mL and so on?

vii) Remember past mistakes you have made and check to see if you have made them again.

viii)   Can the examiner read your answers and working?

ix)   Have you given reasons where necessary?

x)   Have you put all the information on your diagrams?

In essay exams:

i)   Reread each essay - check for spelling errors

ii)   Check your grammar - poor grammar can lead to ambiguous answers.

Moses was the daughter of Pharaoh's son

iii)   Have you answered the question which has been asked? Or have you answered the question that you would like to have been on the exam paper?

iv)   Redo each essay in point form. This helps you check for points that you have left out. Leave your points on the exam paper, where the examiner can read them.

v)   Have you made statements without an argument to back them up?

vi)   Are your quotes correct and have you acknowledged them?

100 Study Tips that Work!

vii) Is your writing legible?

viii) What were your teacher's criticisms in previous tests? Have you made the same errors again?

ix) What did you learn from talking to friends after the last exams? Did someone tell you an idea that you could use now?

x) Mentally review the material that you studied. Did you see a video, read an article or some such, which you could incorporate into your answers now?

TIP 16

What if time is running out in an essay exam?

Write your answer in point form. These may be the exact points that you studied or perhaps the points that you would write if you had the time. You may be penalised for answering in this way, but always bear in mind: If you leave a question blank, you will get zero!! If you don't, you may get a mark for this idea and a mark for that diagram.

What not to do: Don't write a letter to the examiner: *"I really enjoyed this course. Unfortunately, I can't remember the answer to this question, but it was a really great course and you are a really great teacher"*.

And don't tell them that you are running out of time. If you write nonsense like that, of course you'll run out of time!!

100 Study Tips that Work!

TIP 17

Get help as soon as you have a problem

If you are so confused about a topic that you don't know what question to ask, then someone must teach the topic to you again. It is most unlikely that you will understand any topic the first time. Perhaps not even the second time. If you've ever watched a baby trying to walk, you'll know what I mean:

They try and they fall over. They try again and fall over again. They cry in frustration. But they try again. And soon, they are walking, running and maybe representing their country at the Olympics!

That's the way we all learn new things. We try and fail until eventually we get it right. Don't expect to master a topic the first time. Get help NOW!!

Aim high and don't get discouraged.

TIP 18

Any fool can think of a reason not to study

Make studying a habit. Don't let anything interfere with it as you will soon develop bad habits in its place. Look on problems as challenges. OK I'm dying of the flu! What can I do so that my routine is affected minimally? If you don't try, if you let the flu win, then next time it's just that little bit easier to find another reason not to study. Remember: there are many, many reasons - valid reasons - not to study. **But there are no excuses!** Where there's a will there's a way.

TIP 19

Psych yourself up

Think of the things that will adversely affect your study. Now think of how to avoid them. Think of the good things that will flow from your study: fame, fortune, glory!

And practise being a student. If other people don't want to work - OK that's their choice. But you - well you're a student! Students work first and play afterwards, so "No thanks, I won't come to the party: I have work to do." The more you behave like a student, the easier it will become.

TIP 20

Exams should terrify you!

If you aren't terrified of exams, you don't understand their significance. Make your fear work for you. Imagine yourself after your course has finished. Can you see yourself, successful, happy, ready to take on the world? That *can* be you. You must work, you must study, you must put off many of the things that you enjoy doing. But you *can* be that person you want to be. And remember, going through all the pain for a year, will make you a year older with a certificate showing that you can:

- ✓ **Master a subject**
- ✓ **Resist the temptations not to do well**
- ✓ **Organise your time and effort**
- ✓ **Accept responsibility**
- ✓ **Adopt the right attitude for success**
- ✓ **Work under extreme pressure**
- ✓ **Overcome fear and panic**
- ✓ **Master yourself**

These are the things that you need to know about yourself. They are also the things that other people need to know about you - people like friends, family and employers.

But if you don't put the effort in, you'll still be a year older, but with nothing to show for it!

TIP 21

Practice alone, won't make perfect

Mathematics teachers in particular, tell you that all you need is practice. That is just not true. What if you do all the practice but then don't revise. All that you learned will soon be forgotten! What if you practise problems from a poorly written textbook? And yes, they do exist. The problems that you practise may be poorly chosen. They may not cover the entire course. They may be repetitious.

Here are some more things that go with practice:

>You'll need a summary of the course

>You'll need lists of things that you need to know - formulae and so on

>You'll need the best worked examples you can find

>You'll need a revision program so you don't forget what you've learned

>You'll need a list of your mistakes so you know where to take greater care

>You'll need a study timetable and a revision timetable

>You'll need a set of goals

>And *yes* - you'll need **lots and lots of practice**.

TIP 22

Don't fool yourself

If you are to study well, you'll find that it's hard! Hence, don't worry if you don't understand a topic, ask someone to help! Don't think that your problems will go away. They won't. And worse still, tomorrow's ideas will build on the work you didn't understand today. And you won't understand them either!

Soon you'll be saying "I can't do chemistry, or mathematics or history or whatever". What you mean is "I shouldn't have fooled myself - I should have asked for help!"

TIP 23

Yes but I don't have good teachers!

OK it would be good to have the world's best teachers. But the secret of exam success is 10% teaching and 90% hard work. Your school provides the teaching.

You provide the hard work!

And if this course is going to be worthwhile, you had better learn something right now: Don't blame other people. And don't prepare excuses for failure. Failure is failure. Perhaps 95% of your time should have been spent on hard work.

TIP 24

Take responsibility

You - no-one else - are in control of your destiny. *You* will get the glory. *You* will take the blame. Your teacher may be the worst in the world. So what? That means you are going to have to do it without the help of that teacher.

Are there other teachers at your school who can help?
Find them.

Should I hire a teacher outside of the school?
Do so.

Are there books that I can find to help?
Go and look.

Even if your teacher is the best in the world, *you* still have to do the work -
not your teacher.

You will be the one sitting for the exam -
not your teacher.

And you will be the one who succeeds or fails in your life!

Not your teacher.

And what about the others in your class? There are people around you who started studying ages ago. They're so much better than you. How can you hope to compete with them?

The answer is *you can* - and *you will!*

It's the first step that is the hardest. Decide to compete. Plan your attack. And go!

TIP 25

I get really fed up with studying

That's right. Most people - most serious people - do. Studying can do that to you. Your job is to overcome any negative emotions - or at least learn to live with them.

Perhaps the first thing to do is to get out of your room. That's right - go and do something else. Go for a walk. Join a gym. Play tennis. Go to the movies - comedies are best. Look up old friends. See your cousin who left school a couple of years ago and can give you a different perspective on life and study. Remember that students are inside for so much of the time that they may see the sun only occasionally. Sunshine and fresh air are a must for students.

Next, it's time to examine the basics: coffee and junk food are not what your body needs. It's just possible

that you should eat a balanced diet. Ask your doctor about vitamins. I promise you that doctors have met this problem before: students never eat correctly. Students never have enough exercise. Students never have enough sleep. Hence, students always get fed up. Sorry, but it's part of what you do for a living. Remember that there are also rewards for all your grief. They just take longer to materialise.

100 Study Tips that Work!

TIP 26

Plan your work then work your plan

Each of your subjects will be studied in a different way.

In kinesiology, you must know what each muscle looks like and what it does.

In science you must be able to do something different and for mathematics, something different again.

Essay writing needs different skills than, say, geography.

Hence it's important for you to have a plan of attack for each subject. You should know - in advance - when the tests for each subject are to occur: preparing for a single test will be different from the preparation for a half-yearly exam - when all subjects are tested.

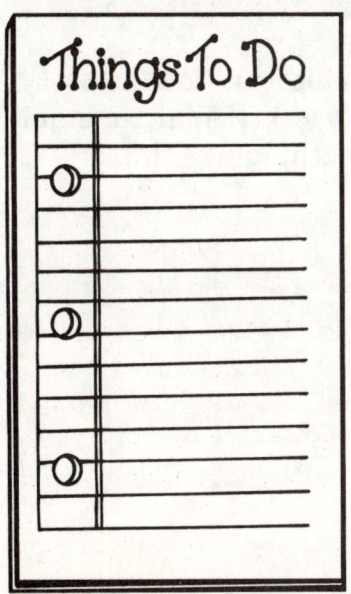

You should find out what books, tapes and videos are available for each subject. If there are Web sites covering your topic, you must seek them out. You must ask if there are any assignments or papers that must be written during the course. Researching and writing assignments will disturb your normal routine - not that students can count on having a "normal" routine.

100 Study Tips that Work!

Once you have all the data, you must plan your work. This means timetabling your entire year, then each term or semester, then each month and finally each week. Use a wall calendar for the long term ones - mid term exams, dates of assignments or excursions, and so on. You can add things to the calendar as you are told them: dates of class tests, etc. Setting up the calendar should take about 10 minutes, no more, including putting it on your wall.

Your monthly and weekly timetables will take longer. But don't spend more than an hour on each. Because of the nature of the world, these will have to be changed from time to time : It rains during the athletics carnival and the carnival is rescheduled for the following week just when you expected to go to the library to complete an assignment. Sorry, but your weekly timetable must be changed.

Or perhaps you find that you have been too ambitious. You need more than 4 hours sleep a night. OK change your timetable.

But, if your friend rings up to invite you to take an afternoon off to go to a game, ***forget it***! Your timetable can be changed, but not for something like this.

TIP 27

Set your parents to work

You'll be in school when the shops are open. So how do you get calendars, books and so on? Get your parents to help. Perhaps they can buy the calendar from the newsagent or get books from the library. Don't let the fact that you can't get to shops provide you with an excuse not to do things. Without help, it is almost impossible for you to work your plan.

And if your parents are willing, why not get them to read the novel you are studying. Not only do you then have someone to talk to about the novel, but often their experience can help with the interpretation of it. This is especially so if you are studying the classics. The language used can often lead to poor understanding of the novel. An adult's ideas may be just the thing you need.

100 Study Tips that Work!

TIP 28

How to fool your parents

Propping 3 or 4 books open on your desk may fool your parents into thinking you are studying. But open books don't mean that you're learning!

Or there is the video: your History teacher tells you about this fantastic World War 2 video. Get the video out from the shop and watch it as many times as you like. As long as there is the sound of bombs and gunfire coming from your room, your parents will know that you are studying! Perhaps the guy in the video shop can recommend other World War 2 films!

There are lots of other ways you can fool parents. If you look hard you can probably find a university study that proves that students learn more if they have a TV on in their room while studying. Or that junk food promotes the growth of brain cells. Show these studies to your parents. They may convince them that you should have junk food and TV.

But there is one person that won't be fooled by this nonsense. And that person is you!! Don't kid yourself!! Don't even try to kid yourself!!!

TIP 29

The Internet will save me

The Net promises everything! But as far as a student is concerned it can be the greatest time waster of all. Parents don't know anything about the Net so they'll encourage you to use it. You'll hear them talking to their friends "Education is so much harder these days. Little Jomo had to spend 11 hours on the Net last night trying to get the information for his test tomorrow. Education is so hard these days!"

Yeah, well, what little Jomo didn't tell his parents was that the material was covered in class, the material is also covered in his textbook, and if little Jomo had spent half an hour reading the summary at the end of the chapter, he could have completed his preparation within an hour!

And, yes, the Net can give you information quickly and easily. Just make sure that you use it correctly. If need be, see if you can find a 6 hour course designed specifically to help students use the Internet. This is an investment of 6 of your precious hours, but it may save you hundreds of hours in the future.

TIP 30

But I don't enjoy studying

You've been taught (brainwashed) that if you are not enjoying yourself, then something is wrong. This is at the core of most students' problems. What you must realise is that much of your life as a student will be hard, joyless work!!

There is nothing wrong if you don't like what you are doing. *It still has to be done!*

There is nothing wrong if you are bored. *Your work will not do itself!*

There is nothing wrong if you are furious that you can't go out with your friends. *Stop complaining and get on with the job at hand!*

This is studying we are talking about! It is *not* entertainment and you should never expect it to be entertaining. Welcome to the world!

100 Study Tips that Work!

TIP 31

The greatest invention - ever!!

No it's not the computer. It's not satellites. It's not even sliced bread. It's pencil and paper!!

Think about it: Every great idea, every piece of literature, mathematics, science and even every movie script was recorded and developed with pencil and paper. All the progress, all the advances in medicine, all of the improvements in the quality of our lives are made possible by writing things down. Years later, sometimes thousands of years later, those same ideas may change the world!

A good example is the study of Conic Sections. The Greeks studied them 2500 years ago. Their ideas were written down, studied and developed until the 20th century when they were used to build satellite dishes. Now we watch television programs from the other side of the world using ideas written down millennia ago.

Our job is to remember things. Normal people forget things easily. We cannot afford to be normal! Write down what you learn!! Use the greatest invention ever!!

100 Study Tips that Work!

TIP 32

My Night-Before-the-Next-Exam-Book

You are not sitting for the Big Exam this afternoon. You are *preparing* to sit for it.

Take appropriate action:

Start a ***Night-Before-the-Next-Exam-Book*** in which you record only those ideas that will get you marks in the next exam. The type of thing I mean is:

i) Mistakes that you have made plus their corrections. The mistakes are as important as the corrections.

ii) Standard questions that you've found.

iii) Typical exam questions. These will occur again and again in future exams.

iv) Odd statements said to you by friends. Remember that knowledge is where you find it. The person alongside of you at school might tell you the best study idea ever. Unless you make a note of this idea, it will disappear forever.

At the end of your course, your Night-Before-Book should contain everything you need for the Big Exam.

How do students ever think they can pass exams without one!!!

100 Study Tips that Work!

TIP 33

Who said you can't study maths?

Of course you can study mathematics. That's what your Night-Before-Book is for. Once a week or so, read it and update it. It doesn't take long, and you'll find that your confidence and ability increase at once.

And yes, you must do lots of questions as well. But in order to be able to do the questions, you must know things: formulae, techniques, standard questions, properties of shapes and graphs. All of these should be in your Night-Before book so that each time you open it, you see something which will be worth marks to you in the next exam.

TIP 34

Put things in lists

If you have to learn something, it's easier to learn if you make up a list. Hence make lists of things and number them. For example, say that you have to know the properties of triangles. First, make a list of the types of triangles:

1   Scalene triangles

2   Isosceles triangles

3   Equilateral triangles

4   Acute angled triangles

5   Obtuse angled triangles

6   Right angled triangles

Now you know that there are only six types of triangles, you know how much effort you'll need to learn them. On the other hand, if you have to learn the first fifty elements in Chemistry, you'll have to spend more time in learning them - maybe even develop a different *method* of learning them. But in either case, by putting the things to be known in a list, you know

1   what they are

2   how difficult it will be to learn them

100 Study Tips that Work!

TIP 35

Bite sized bits

Break your tasks up into little bits. Don't say "Tonight I'm going to study Mathematics." Say, "Tonight I'm going to learn the properties of quadrilaterals".

Hence your first job for the night should take you about 20 minutes to half an hour. At the end of that time, you should have found the properties, made a list of them in your Night-Before-Book and perhaps started to memorise them. In other words, you have successfully completed something important within 20 minutes. Now try for another 20 minutes on the topic in History from Term 1 that always worried you. You now know what to do. You have 20 minutes in which to do it. See how you go.

An old principle says that if you have 20 minutes in which to complete a task, you'll complete it in the 20 minutes. But, if you have 2 hours in which to complete the same task, guess what, you'll take 2 hours.

TIP 36

Learn the formulae first

A good text book will have a list of any formulae used in each chapter. So, a Business Studies text may have, at the end of the Finance chapter:

List of formulae used in this chapter

1. Simple Interest $\quad I = \dfrac{Pnr}{100}$

2. Compound Interest $\quad A = PR^n$

3. Repayment on standard loan

$$M = \dfrac{PR^N(R-1)}{R^N - 1}$$

4. Amount in superannuation fund

$$S = \dfrac{PR(R^N - 1)}{R - 1}$$

Before you study this chapter, learn the formulae! It will make reading and studying the chapter much easier, if you don't have to keep referring back to the formulae.

TIP 37

Feeling at home with your Night-Before book

In writing your Night-Before-Book, make each page look the same. Put the references at the top of each page, the facts in a box on the right hand side, the quotes in a box on the left and so on. It makes it easier to find the quotes, say, if you know where on the page they will be found. It's like knowing where the furniture is in your home.

TIP 38

Do it now and save a row

Summaries and revision notes must be prepared during the year. Your Night-Before-Book is to be *studied*, not written, on the night before the exam. And remember, there are a million reasons not to do it now, but there are no excuses!

Think to yourself: The reason people get so worried about exams is probably that they are not well prepared. They leave their preparation till the last moment - hoping that the end of the world will come before their exam. Well, the end of the world may come. But you'd have to be very lucky for it to come just before your exam.

There are two types of worry:

Productive Worry

and **Unproductive Worry**

Persons with Productive Worry take precautions. They know that they must prepare, so they prepare. They know that there is work that must be done. So they start working. And yes, they are worried, but they use their worry as a driving force to make them work harder.

Persons with Unproductive Worry are also worried. But they don't do anything productive about it. They talk to their friends - sometimes for hours - about how worried they are. They worry about how much work must be done - but they never think to do anything about it. They worry that they are not good enough to do this course - and as time goes by, they get closer and closer to being correct. These people use their worry as a topic of conversation and, eventually, as an excuse for doing nothing about it.

TIP 39

I know it now, but I'll never remember it!!

That's normal. Your job as a student is to learn how to remember. For example:

When you learn something, don't expect to remember it: Write it down!! The best place to write it is in your Night-Before-Book, but as a temporary measure, use your school diary or anything.

When you take notes, you'll find the little things, the tricks, the pieces of advice given by the teacher, really do help you understand and remember. Don't just write down the main heading: write down as much as possible. If you don't, you'll have to do the whole topic again. What a waste of time!

TIP 40

Talking about your Diary

Use your school diary for revision. If you have a formula or technique that you keep forgetting, put it in your diary on the 5th of each month, say. Then on the 5th you have an **Automatic Memory Boost.**

TIP 41

Good memory = Great effort

Here's a true story: I go to a party and get introduced to someone:

"John Smith", they say. "That's an easy name to remember."

Ten minutes later, they can't remember my name to save their souls. Why? Well it certainly is an easy name to remember, and because of that, they don't make any *effort* to remember it. They assume that since it is such an easy name, it will "be remembered" by magic in some part of their brain. And that same series of events has happened to me a thousand times. I'll bet that Arnold Schwarzenegger has never had that happen:

"Arnold who?" they'd say. "Schwarzenegger. How do you spell that? No, wait a moment, I'll have to see Schwarzenegger written down. How do you spell it? OK I've got it. Arnold Schwarz-en-egger. Boy, what a great name!"

And they remember Arnold's name forever - because they invested time and effort in remembering it.

The same applies to your studies. You will not remember unless you invest your time and effort.

TIP 42

Remembering short lists

There are many different techniques that people use in order to remember a list of things:

Some people have to see things written down.

Others have to hear them aloud.

Others have to talk about them to other people.

Others learn best if they can touch things - one student I know uses children's alphabet blocks to spell out the things to be remembered.

In general, the best advice is to use as many techniques as possible. Some techniques will suit you better than others. Use them all until you find the one that is best for you.

TIP 43

Using Key-words to remember

When you were in the lower grades, everyone tried to learn essays word for word. As you became better, you should have realised that it was only the key ideas that needed to be remembered. You could fill in the gaps yourself.

By now, you should be ready to get down to key words. If the first paragraph of the essay you want to remember concerns Caesar's rise to power, you may only need to remember the words Family, Army and Expectations to remind you of the main points of the entire paragraph. Altogether you may have to remember only 8 or 9 words to cover the entire essay.

100 Study Tips that Work!

TIP 44

The List of Ten method

For lists of things up to 10 items, some people use the following method:

Firstly learn the table:

1	- sun	6	- sticks
2	- shoe	7	- heaven
3	- tree	8	- gate
4	- door	9	- wine
5	- hive	10	- hen

These are easy to recall because they rhyme with their numbers.

Now, say you have to remember the following points. Let's say they are the key-words of a History essay that you are expecting to get in an exam:

1	Putty	6	Army
2	Power	7	Generals
3	Murder	8	Civil war
4	Enemy	9	Death
5	Consolidation	10	Democracy

These 10 are not so easy to learn. So we associate the two lists:

100 Study Tips that Work!

The first word "sun" is associated with the word "putty". Think of a situation connecting the two words: you are carrying a huge pile of putty in both hands. It's a very hot day. You can feel the sun beating down on you. Suddenly you notice that the putty is getting soft because of the sun's heat. It starts to melt, running through your fingers, splashing down on your boots. Try to imagine yourself in the scene. And try to make the scene as silly as possible. Silly things are easier to remember. Make the sun into a living thing, calling out abuse to the putty. But try to associate the easy-to-remember word "sun" with the difficult-to-remember word "putty".

Now do the same with the next two words "shoe" and "power". Once you have associated the first five with the other five, go back and see if you can recall all five. If you can, continue with the remaining words. If you can't, go back and reinforce the ones you can't remember. Make your association story more ridiculous, emphasise the two words you want to associate and so on. Once you have finished, test yourself for the entire list. Then see if you can say the list backwards. Get someone to call out numbers at random and see if you can give the corresponding word from the list. With very little practice you'll find that you can remember any list of 10 or less words in minutes.

People have refined and adapted this technique to suit whatever they have to learn. If you wanted to remember the number 3.14159, you could first change it into tree, sun, door, sun, hive, wine from our standard list, and then make up a story: *"I was climbing a tree in order to reach the sun, when I saw a door in mid-air. Through it I could see the sun peering out of an enormous hive . The bees were singing and I realised they were drunk on honey wine.."* Use your imagination and practise this technique.

TIP 45

Learning longer lists

If you want to learn longer lists, you can certainly adapt the List of 10 method. Or perhaps you can make up a sentence each word of which starts with the first letter of the words in the list. A common one for the planets of the Solar System is *Men Very Easily Make Jugs Serve Useful Needs and Pleasures*. You will find mnemonics (memory aiding devices) for the first 100 elements in Chemistry in many books. But it's better to make up your own.

However, don't waste your time. Ask yourself whether it is worth your while learning a list of the 100 elements of Chemistry. What sort of exam question would need that sort of knowledge?

TIP 46

Using Key Words in exams

Because you only have a short time in an exam, you must be quick. But often you will try to save time by reading the questions quickly. When that happens, you will often misread questions and hence lose marks.

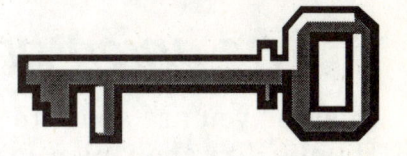

Obviously, you must slow down. But that is sometimes easier said than done. Use the Key Words technique: Underline the important words in the question before you start. To do this you will have to slow down and read each question carefully. Take this question from a Year 9 maths test as an example:

Find the compound interest on a deposit of $485 invested at 1% per month over 6 years.

After reading and underlining it, this question may look like this:

Find the compound interest on a deposit of $485 invested at 1% per month over 6 years.

Someone else may jot notes down on the question:

Not just amount
Subtract principal

Principal

Find the compound interest on a deposit of $485 invested at 1% per month over 6 years.

r = 0.01

change to months

It's not very neat but it's achieved its purpose of slowing you down. As a bonus, you've identified the trick of changing years into months and that the question is asking for the interest not the accumulated amount.

TIP 47

The onion principle

Imagine you are about to start studying Hamlet. Try the Onion Principle and see if it doesn't speed up your understanding and enjoyment.

The Onion Principle simply means that you start from the outside and gradually work your way in. Like this:

1. Ask someone what Hamlet is. They will laugh at you for being so silly. *"Hamlet is a person, Stupid. Boy, how dumb can you get?!"* That's OK. Let them laugh. You don't intend to remain stupid.

2. Find someone who can tell you about Hamlet.

100 Study Tips that Work!

Who is he? Sorry, who was he? Was he a real person? When did he live? And so on. These are just general questions. But they help prepare your mind for the real thing later on.

3   Try and find a summary of the play - yes by now you've figured out it's a play. Read the summary and try to imagine what the scenery would be like. Ask general questions of yourself. Do I like Hamlet? Does he sound like a good guy? What about his relatives? Use your imagination!

4   Now would be a good time to talk to someone who did this course last year. Anyone who knows the play will do - but steer clear of experts. The more you talk about the play, the more your curiosity will be aroused. and the more you will feel that you know the characters. Someone will tell you that the person who wrote the play lived 400 odd years ago. He wrote other plays as well.

5   Apparently this play is really well known. Look in a book of quotations and see if there are any quotes listed from Hamlet. What about other plays by Shakespeare?

6   Give your video dealer a call and see if anyone has made a film of Hamlet. If you can find it, watch it - perhaps with a friend. Afterwards, talk about the video.

7   By now you should know about as much as you can without actually reading the play. When you start studying the play in class, you will find that your understanding of it allows you to read and enjoy it far more than if you had just heard of it for the first time.

You can use the Onion Principle in every subject, with very few modifications.

TIP 48

Learn things by heart

Many teachers insist that you "understand" topics. Because they stress understanding, many teachers frown on learning things by heart. Some teachers try to get you to "understand" why six sevens are 42. You will see their students in later life reaching for a calculator in order to multiply by 10. The speed with which these students can do their maths exams is so slow that they can't finish the paper. Teachers then complain that these students don't understand what they are doing.

Don't let this happen to you. Learn your tables. Learn the causes of the First World War. Learn as many facts as you can!

And when you know your facts, you can then start wondering why events occurred in the way they did. Would a slight change here produce a huge change there? Or you may wonder why the sum of the odd numbers is always a perfect square ($1 + 3 + 5 = 3^2$, and so on). You may even wonder about a formula from dynamics:

$$mx'' = mg - mkv$$ looks so much like a formula from electricity: $$Li' = E - Ri$$

And of course you should try to understand the things that you have learned. But how can you understand something that you haven't learned? You must know "what" before you can ask "why?"

TIP 49

The knee bone's connected to the thigh bone

In a sense, everything is connected to everything else. Always look back over what you have just learned. See if there is a connection between what you learned and your own experiences.

Perhaps you've been studying how Hitler took over Czechoslovakia. The text book might say: *"On the 16th of March in 1939 Hitler invaded Czechoslovakia."* That doesn't really jump off the page at you. It certainly doesn't help you understand the effect this invasion had on the Czechs. But now reread it. What in your experience would be like this? Well, what about your brother? He always comes into your room, invades your privacy, looks through your diary. He's a real pain and you'd like to ....

OK, now look back at Hitler. How would you expect the Czechs to react? They can't tell their parents - they have to do something themselves. But, wouldn't they be angry!! Now look at the next paragraph in your book. It's labelled "The rise of the Resistance Movement." Well of course it is! This wouldn't surprise you at all. You'd probably go on and read that paragraph out of interest, now that you know how the Czechs felt. Who knows, you may get a couple of ideas on what to do with your brother.

Make a habit of making connections. The more you make, the more interesting the subject becomes - and - the easier it is to remember.

TIP 50

Don't tell me what to do!!

Everybody talks about Discipline being important. And they're right ! But they probably mean something different from what you mean.

Discipline starts with your parents saying "*Don't do this, don't do that*". But your parents don't expect to be there forever, telling you what to do and what not to do. They expect *you* to start doing the right thing yourself. *You* are supposed to stop yourself from doing wrong. And you're meant to be able to discipline yourself in all things. The original list of Don'ts was just to get you started.

Mature adults are people who can discipline themselves, people who can resist peer pressure, who don't say "*Yes*" when they know they should say "*No*".

The common name for people who do this is "COOL".

TIP 51

But I do need help!!

And in any case, the study business is about learning things. Your maxim should be: Please tell me what I should know, how to learn it, how to remember it and how to reproduce it. Once you've been told, you can then decide whether to follow the advice or not. But first get the advice!!

And, you can find advice anywhere: your parents, teachers, friends, books, videos - all of these may have the advice that you need. We all seem to wait for Experts to give us the Secrets of Life. We hang on their every word and usually come away disappointed. But a chance conversation with a student in the corridor may give you the insights that you hoped to get from the experts.

Listen to what people say to you. Think about what they meant. Talk to friends about anything you learned. People who were failures at school may be able to tell you why they failed. People who succeeded at school may have hints that you can use.

When I was at school a maths teacher said to a student who had not done his homework, that he, the teacher, used to do hundreds of maths questions when he was at school. He did not say it as if it were a Great Truth that he had discovered, but just as general classroom conversation. Now, that was the first time that any of us realised that hard work was needed for success - harder work than we had ever expected!

And if you took notice of that piece of advice, your life would go in one direction and if you didn't take that advice you would go in a totally different direction.

TIP 52

The more you talk, the easier it becomes

Talk about your work and what you have learned with your friends. We learn best by using our knowledge. Explaining what you have learned, forces you to review it, to repackage it and to recite it. If you do a good job, you will get questions from your friends which you must answer. This causes you to think deeply about your work, to reinforce it and to imprint it on your memory.

But it's *talk about work* that's important - not talk which is idle gossip. Walk away from *"Then I said this and then he said that"* conversations.

TIP 53

Problems, problems, problems

In mathematics and science, much of your work will be solving problems. Always try to do three examples of the same type:

The first will introduce you to the new words and ideas needed.

The second will get you used to how these ideas are put together.

The third allows you to try one yourself - your answer to this one should be perfect!

Then write up what you have found, together with the techniques needed, in your Night-Before-Book.

TIP 54

Looking back over what you've learned

Once you've learned something, mentally review it. Step back from your books and see where this new piece of knowledge fits in. For example: say you have just learned that while the Romans were conquering the known world, they didn't have domestic problems. But when the known world was conquered, then the Empire gradually fell apart with domestic strife.

OK, I understand that. Now let's see if that fits into my knowledge base: I wonder if that's where America is today? I wonder that with no more worlds left to conquer, we could expect domestic strife to increase? I wonder if the Barbarians are about to invade and destroy? How could I find out?

While you are thinking about this you are reinforcing your knowledge of history and are indeed using your knowledge of history to help you understand the world today. Who knows where your speculations will lead you?

TIP 55

Mistakes are teachers too!

Often you'll see students tear up an exam paper because they are ashamed or angry at the mark they have received. If you glance at their paper you will see the examiner's comments all over the paper.

And they tear it up!!???

This is an extremely important document. It is ideal for your study purposes. The marker has just shown you which parts of your course you didn't understand!!

The examiners are saying to you: *If you can fix these mistakes, you must get 100% !!*

Once you have received your exam paper back you should do the following:

1. Analyse your mistakes carefully.

2. Find out the correct method of answering that question.

3. Write up your mistakes in your Night-Before-Book - together with comments.

4. Practise several other questions of the same type.

TIP 56

What you don't prepare will be in the next exam

Always work on the assumption that if you don't fix a mistake right now - you will get it in your next exam for sure.

Think of mistakes as being like a flat tyre. Yes, you can drive a car with a flat tyre. But you will have to drive very slowly and if you travel too far on a flat tyre, you will cause permanent damage to your car.

So too, if you don't fix your mistakes, your understanding of new topics may be slowed down, and eventually you may not understand the next topic at all.

TIP 57

Maths and the subconscious mind

We have two types of sight. The first tells us about the world. We use it to read, we use it for looking around and it's the one we use consciously. The second type of sight allows us to move about in the world without tripping over things. This second one works even when we aren't thinking about it. It works automatically.

When you attack a maths problem, there should also be two parts of your brain involved. The first is the automatic one: it draws a diagram, writes down a formula, and substitutes into it without your having to think about it. Then the other part of your brain takes over and tries to solve the question.

You have to develop these two parts of your brain. With practice, you should be drawing diagrams, writing down formulae and so on as automatically as you can navigate a room.

TIP 58

Practise thinking while people are talking

This is sometimes called Active Listening.

If you use it during a lesson or when someone is explaining something to you, you'll find that you can understand and remember with greater ease.

Think about what is being said. In class, ask yourself:

> I wonder if she's right?
>
> That may be so, but could there be another explanation?
>
> Does his evidence prove what he claims?
>
> That reminds me of some other topic. Is there a connection?
>
> But a few minutes ago she said ....

Keep asking yourself these questions. As soon as you find something that you don't understand, ask the teacher what is meant. Write down the answer - remember that normal people will have forgotten the answer within minutes. And, with practice, you will start asking questions that are *related* to what is being said. Continue making your notes and continue asking your questions - *sensible* questions, until they make you stop.

TIP 59

You are losing marks if you believe this

"I knew my work. I just made Careless Errors"

How many times have you said or thought this? "Careless Errors" means that you can't do anything about them. They are not really your fault. You can't be held responsible for them since everyone makes them.

No! No! No!!!

There is no such thing as a Careless Error! If you diligently write them down in your Night-Before-Book, you will soon see that there are certain patterns in your Careless Errors. You may find that you are reading the question too fast. You may find that you are assuming what the question is going to say, rather than reading it carefully and then reading it again and then reading it and underlining the key-words. Once you can see the pattern in your "Careless" errors, you can start doing something about avoiding them.

TIP 60

Classify your Mistakes

When you get your corrected paper back from the teacher, use this table to analyse your mistakes. While all mistakes are important, some are easier to fix than others, some are costing you more marks than others and so on. This table can help you know which mistake is which. If you know of any other techniques which will help, add them to the list.

Type of Mistake	What it cost me in marks	What I can do to fix it
I thought I knew this topic		
I didn't know this topic was in the exam		
I didn't learn this topic		
I didn't understand this topic		
I didn't know the facts		
I didn't give references		
I misread the question		
I didn't include quotes		
I didn't draw a diagram		
I left out part of the question accidentally		
I didn't check my working		
I didn't label the diagram		
I wasn't neat - the teacher couldn't read my answer		
I made mistakes through lack of time		
I made "careless" errors		

TIP 61

How to make a success of your day

Try planning your day. Make a list of what you want to achieve today. Don't make the list so long that you can't possibly complete it. But, your list should be long enough that you feel a sense of achievement when you have finished. Persist in making up your list each day. Eventually you will find that your list is so long that you can't believe that you will finish it. And yet you will!

Don't underestimate the buzz you get from completing this list of tasks. It's a way of giving yourself a pat on the back - each day. It's also a great way of managing your time.

TIP 62

Worst things first

Any list of things to do will contain some things that you hate to do and others that you love to do. Do the hateful ones first!! It's like washing up versus going out: do the washing up first! Then the only things left to do are things you enjoy. On the other hand, if you put off doing the hateful things, you will contrive to run out of time before you have a chance to start them - and you have another wasted day.

TIP 63

How to find an extra hour in the day

As soon as you start making a daily list of things you want to do and study, you will start noticing gaps in your day. Say that it takes you 30 minutes on the train to get to school. Usually you have

- i) looked out the window
- ii) read the paper
- iii) talked to someone

All of these may be important to you. They may be important for your mental and personal well being. But the fact remains: there is a 30 minute period which you could use for study. Now, if you decide to keep this 30 minute period as it is, then you should class it as leisure time and put it on your timetable.

And what about the journey home? You have another half hour there. And between your afternoon session and dinner there is a 15 minute gap. And at lunch you might find an extra 20 minutes. And there may be more.

If you can't work at home early in the morning, why not go to school half an hour early. You may be surprised how many other students and teachers are there early. You can spend the extra time in the library or even talking to teachers about your work. You can never speak to teachers throughout the day as everyone is so busy, but in the early morning they are much more approachable.

Become jealous of your time. You have so little of it, so use it wisely.

100 Study Tips that Work!

TIP 64

Homework, revision, study

Homework, revision and study are 3 different tasks. Don't think, as your parents may do, that time spent on homework will ensure success in exams. Your success will come from what you learn from doing your homework and writing up your mistakes and reading around your subject and ....

You may find that the homework set for you is interfering with your revision and study time. Try to build revision into your homework. Always review what you have done in your homework. It will take only minutes, but it will help you remember other parts of the course, you will see how things fit into the whole and how they affect each other.

TIP 65

What about food?

Starting a study session on an empty stomach gives you a perfect reason to stop studying. Be sensible. You can't function for long on an empty stomach. And you can't work after a huge meal. Studying takes energy and you need a steady supply. Hence eat complex carbohydrates before you start - no, they are not chocolates!! Have a piece of fruit and a sandwich on your desk for later.

TIP 66

5 minutes preparation

Before you start your study session, revise what you know and don't know. You can do this in the car or bus on the way home. Then when you do start, you're already warmed up, you're ready to roll! It's like warming up before you play sport.

TIP 67

Use deadlines

If you allow yourself 4 hours in which to write an essay, you will probably take 4 hours. If you allow yourself 1 hour to write the same essay, you will probably take 1 hour. Get into the habit of specifying a time limit for tasks. It will breed a habit of mind in which you start at top speed - and hence will complete the task much faster.

Of course, this does not mean that you sacrifice quality work for speed!

TIP 68

Your timetable

Within school, your day is divided up into periods. Once the science period is over, you start on English. Your time is divided up for you. But, most of your work in the senior school will be done outside class. Hence you must have a study timetable.

You know what a timetable looks like:

You've got seven days, each with 24 hours.

You have 6 subjects to study and each needs a different amount of time.

You need 3 study periods for each subject per week.

You have to sleep, attend school, eat and have a social life.

You have to allow time for visits to the library, the doctor and the dentist.

You have to have exercise and there will be times when you have the flu and can't work.

Just timetable all of these and there you are!

100 Study Tips that Work!

When you write down all the variables, it seems impossible. Here are a few things to bear in mind:

1. Keep as little detail on the timetable as possible. If you are to have a 5 minute break each half hour, then remember it. Don't clutter the timetable up with it.

2. Your timetable will have to be changed during the year. As you master one subject you will have to spend more time on others. Illness, sports carnivals and the like, will disrupt your schedule. Hence, be flexible.

3. Your health is super important. Put your exercise breaks on the timetable.

4. Don't overload the timetable. You will not be able to keep up with unrealistic goals and then your entire study program is in jeopardy.

5. Put in small periods of time rather than large. Two half hour sessions are better than a one hour session.

6. Show rest and leisure periods on the timetable. It's important for you to see what fraction of your week is devoted to study, rest and sleep.

TIP 69

Speak up - it's a family affair

You are part of a team. People are expecting you to do your best. They will feed you, clean up your room, do your washing, drive you to school and a hundred other things as long as you are doing the right thing and are working at your studies. If you need help, you owe it to them to speak up and ask for it. If you don't, then you are letting the team down!

TIP 70

But I can't study tonight!

If you cannot study tonight, have a Reduced Time Program that you can do in your head. Have this already thought out for just such an emergency. Use the time to go over mentally what would have been done if you had been studying at your desk. Often you'll discover something that you don't know as well as you thought you did. When you do get back to your routine, the first thing you do is to revise that topic.

TIP 71

Be consistent!

Your study program can be ruined by many things. The worst is not being consistent. It's like cleaning your teeth: some people don't clean them until they get a toothache. Then they try to make up for lost time by cleaning them every half hour. It doesn't work for teeth and it doesn't work for study.

> **You must study every day.**

TIP 72

Yes but what about a valid excuse?

There aren't any! We've talked about reasons and excuses before. Reasons for missing a study session may be valid, but at best they slow you down. At worst they can stop your progress altogether. We all know people who "just take a year off " school. A year later they "just can't seem to get back into it". Nothing can excuse your missing a study session!

Now, that is not to say that study sessions won't be missed. But you should feel guilty about missing them and you should make up a missed session as soon as you can. You have an obligation to yourself, and those around you, to do your best.

TIP 73

Make your timetable achievable

Consistency's worst enemy is a poorly thought out timetable. If you decide to do 14 hours of study every day, seven days a week you are fooling yourself. You will not be able to achieve it and after one day you will have failed. This negative start to your study program lessens your self esteem and you quickly revert to not studying at all.

Do your studying in bite sized pieces. Set small, achievable goals. And reward yourself when you achieve them.

100 Study Tips that Work!

TIP 74

I know this - I don't need to study it!

As you get better, you will have a different problem: you may not need to study parts of the course as much, so you don't. But you then start to forget what you once knew perfectly. Like this:

I am an idiot.
I don't know
this topic.

So I don't have to study anymore.

So I study and study.

Soon I have mastered the topic.
I am now smart.

It's easy to fix... If you have been studying a subject four times a week reduce it to three or two or one on your timetable. And use the saved time for other subjects.

TIP 75

Light reading

There will be times when you are tired. When you can't look at another textbook. For times like this always have light reading at hand.

What is light reading? This book is light reading!! Any book that can help your mindset is light reading. Other books - Vampire Boy Scouts and so on - are for relaxation. They are fine, but you read them during your timetabled rest periods.

TIP 76

Your worst subject may save your life

Let's say that English is your best subject and that Geography is your worst. Isn't it tempting to spend more time on English? And isn't it tempting to ignore Geography altogether? Don't!! Education is about giving you Choices! Ignoring Geography simply limits your choices. Put in the time on Geography and bring it up to the same level as English.

TIP 77

Goals

Perhaps you don't know what you want to do with your life. That's OK. You do know, however, that studying and passing exams are important. Why else are you reading this book?

So, your long term goal is to succeed in your exams.

But what about short term goals?

What are you going to study tonight?

On your way home, start preparing yourself: First I'll complete the assignment. Then I want to revise Chapter 4 in the Economics book - there's a test on it in 2 weeks. Third, I'll glance over work we did today - that will mean making notes in my Night-Before-the-Exam-Book. Fourth ... and so on. By the time you've reached home you should know what has to be done, how long each task should take, when you will eat and so on.

You may have to adjust your timetable in order to accommodate the day to day changes to your study life. Schools are very unpredictable places. A class test may be sprung for tomorrow and your timetable cannot predict that. Hence, you may have to temporarily change your timetable just because of the nature of schools.

100 Study Tips that Work!

TIP 78

Goals for after your exams

On the other hand, perhaps you have goals for after your exams. These long term goals are even more valuable:

Write down these long term goals. Keep them in mind by reviewing them often. Make them part of your personality. Then when the temptation is to take the night off, or to sleep in on a cold morning, your list of goals can give you the jolt you need: I *do* want to succeed! I am *not* the sort of person who slacks around!

Make them as corny as you like. They are not for publication: they are part of your self motivation and you'll be surprised how well they will work for you.

If you don't have goals for after your final exams, that's OK as well. If you want to try to get some, ask yourself what you'd *really* like to be doing in 5 years time. Then backtrack and see if you can imagine what steps you'd have to take to get from here to there. If this works for you, you now have a long term goal. Remember that if it doesn't work, that's still OK. It would be silly to make up a false, long term goal just so you can say that you have one.

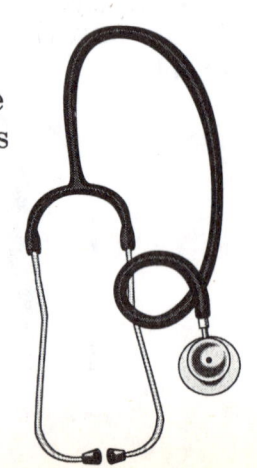

TIP 79

Set small goals

OK so you'd like to get 100% in the final exam. We all would. But your goal can't be achieved all at once. Set yourself Small Goals. They are easier to achieve, you get a boost of self confidence each time you achieve them, and gradually you get closer to your ultimate 100% goal.

Remember that it is easier to give 100% effort and concentration on achieving a Small Goal whereas you may feel daunted by a large one.

For instance, if your goal is to master algebra, study the rules for factorisation tonight, i.e. learn what they are, how to use them, and then practise them.

Frequent breaks are important for concentration. Hence study for 20 minutes - then have a break. This forces you to have goals that can be achieved in 20 minutes. Your timetable should reflect this.

And, the added bonus is that studying in short bursts lets your brain stay alert for the entire task.

TIP 80

The odd 5 minutes

Practise using small amounts of time.

If you have 15 minutes before your favourite TV show, use that time to read over your Latin vocab or your trig formulae.

If you have 20 minutes, write an essay on a topic that you have not researched. In 10 minutes you can start to outline the sketch you must do for Design and Tech. In 5 minutes you can look up the meaning of the word *synergy* for Science.

If you use these short time periods, that will leave more time for relaxation. If you don't, then you will have to find more time from somewhere else.

TIP 81

Categorise your work

In planning your study, group your work into types:

1. Work that takes 10 minutes - to use between dinner and your favourite TV show

2. Work you can revise mentally during the trip to school

3. Major topics which need 30 minutes or more

4. Research topics that mean a trip to a library in a search of an encyclopedia or the Net.

TIP 82

Nobody wants to be a fool!

Of course they don't! But you'd never know with some people. They will sit in a class trying to look as if they know and understand everything. But they don't. No-one understands everything. But there they sit, never asking for help. Never asking anything. Just sitting. And why? Because they think that other people will think them a fool if they ask a question.

Remember: It is better to be *thought* a fool for a minute by asking a question, than to *be* a fool for the rest of your life by not asking it.

TIP 83

I don't understand!!

This is the universal cry for help. Just imagine:

You're sitting in class and the teacher is talking about something that he obviously thinks is important. He mentions again and again that what he is explaining is going to

i) be in the exam

ii) be the basis for new work that is coming up

iii) be the answer to all your previous problems in this subject.

Trouble is: you don't understand what he's talking about!!!

100 Study Tips that Work!

What should you do? You can't interrupt - it's not that sort of class. You can't ask a friend what it's about. *Everyone but you* seems to understand. It's like the party that no-one invited you to!!

There are several things you should do.

i) Copy down anything that your teacher is writing on the board.

ii) Write down anything that he is saying that has to do with this topic

iii) Don't worry. School - and life - are full of things that you won't understand the first time. You are copying down all this stuff so that you can study it later. Then you will be able to ask for help on things that were said in class. You can ring your friends, you can ask your parents, you can speak to your teacher about it the next day.

iv) Don't think that other people understand things the first time. They don't. We are all very similar in this regard. We understand after we've practised, made mistakes, and thought about it. The person who claims to be able to understand everything the first time through needs help. Buy him this book!

TIP 84

I do understand - now what?

What do you do if the teacher is going on about something that you already know and understand?

i) Make sure that your summary includes everything that is being said - the fact that you know and understand today doesn't guarantee anything about tomorrow.

ii) Mentally revise the sort of mistakes that you could make under pressure

iii) Try to make connections between this topic and other topics - the more connections that you can make, the better prepared you will be. Say it's the midpoint formula in Mathematics - which you've known since Year 8: You'd expect to see it in questions on co-ordinate geometry but could you get a question needing it in, say,

>Arithmetic? - yes the midpoint formula is an arithmetic mean (average)

>Series and sequences? - yes, if a, b, c are in AP then $b = \dfrac{a + c}{2}$

>Simple Harmonic Motion? - yes to find the centre of motion if you know where it's stopped

>and so on

While you are making these connections, you are also revising the other topics and also learning to expect the unexpected question.

TIP 85

Big things are made up of little things

More than any other subject, Mathematics builds on what has gone before. And more than any other subject, to be good at Mathematics you must enjoy it. And before you can enjoy it, you must know the basics. Ask your teacher for help. Is there another textbook that she can recommend you use? Can she write a revision sheet? Ask questions always. Teachers will help you if they know that you need help and are keen to learn. The smallest, most insignificant question may be vitally important. Get the answer to it as soon as you can.

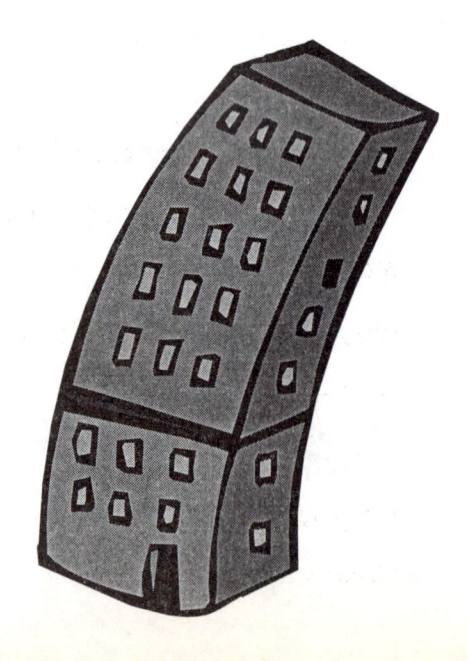

TIP 86

Five W's and an H

Make sure you understand the difference between:

>A quiz show and

>A school

If you are studying for a quiz show you need to know Facts, Facts and more Facts.

In a school you need to know the reasons why things happen. In class, make a habit of asking yourself the Five W's and an H:

>*Who*

>>*What*

>>>*When*

>>>>*Where*

>>>>>*Why*

>>>>>>*How*

Make these questions automatic. Learning a subject is much, much more than learning answers for a quiz.

So if you have to know about the Berlin Wall:

Who built it?

What exactly is it? What is it made of?

When was it built?

Where was it?

Why was it built?

How was it built?

Once you have asked these questions and once you have found out the answers, you can start your further questions:

Are there other walls like the Berlin Wall?

Did the Berlin Wall work?

What did other people think of the Wall?

How long did it stand?

Could you have achieved the same result without building the Wall?

And so on.

TIP 87

Preparing for the next lesson

Obviously, if you miss a lesson you must catch it up. Get on the phone immediately to friends who can tell you what happened, what notes were given and what was said.

But what about tomorrow's lesson?

If you know what the next topic your teacher is going to cover in class, read over that topic before you start it in class. This gives you an overview of the topic. You will be more familiar with the words in that topic - the names of the Kings and Queens, the sorts of formulae you will meet, how long the topic is when compared with other topics.

TIP 88

It's your problem!

If you don't understand the importance of something that the teacher is talking about, take particular notice. Write notes as to what is being said. If the teacher is talking about the types of language used in Hamlet - formal, informal and so on, and you can't see the point of it and you think it's really boring, then you've got the problem!

These ideas are going to be in your exam. These ideas are going to come up again in other parts of the course! These ideas are going to drive you mad in future because you didn't make the effort to understand them! These ideas will change your life and allow you to go into marketing, management, song writing and a million other fields if only you master them today!! It's worth the effort!!!

TIP 89

Where should I study?

I guess that the answer is anywhere that works. But as for your permanent place - it's usually your bedroom. The exception would be if you come from a family that studies together around the dinner table.

Easier to answer is where *not* to study: You can't study successfully in front of the TV. I know that you read about the person who topped the National Exams last year - she didn't do any work except watching television. Sure! The article was in the same paper as that report about the squirrel who reads Shakespeare.

Just forget nonsense stories like these. They don't happen to real people.

You can't do two things at once. Either study for the test OR watch TV. Don't do both.

You will also hear of highly successful people who study with the radio on, or with music playing. The trouble with these stories is that the person would have been highly successful without the radio or music. Listening to music does not make you a successful student! Just a typical one.

So get yourself a desk - the bigger the better and put as many shelves above it as possible. Get a good lamp - you don't want to end up with a great brain and ruined eyes.

If you are unlucky enough to have a computer on your desk - get rid of it. Otherwise your brother and sister will always be coming into your room to use it. Your e-mail will disturb you. A friend will want to play a game over the Net with you and so on. All of these disturb your study. Put the computer somewhere else.

100 Study Tips that Work!

And as for the telephone: not only should you not have one in your room, you should get your parents to screen your calls. If you don't, I'd recommend that you leave school at once. Study is not for you. Become a telephonist if the phone is so necessary for your life.

Everything in your study room and on your desk should be relevant to study. Be totally ruthless in this. Keeping your mind on study is hard enough. Anything that distracts you should be eliminated!

And just to show that you understand about study, put a sign - a big sign - above your desk saying:

> There is no magic wand!
> I'm *all* there is!

TIP 90

Rest and Recreation

You do need rest and recreation. Factor in exercise as part of your study routine. Allow time for recreation - go to places where you can relax and laugh, times when your brain can exercise itself on totally different planes.

And fitness is part of your recreation. Exams are very stressful. Go for a daily walk if nothing else. Get your sleep, otherwise your concentration will suffer.

TIP 91

What about - ugh! - good food?

You don't have to go overboard with good food. But you should take a healthy interest in nutrition. For example, junk food floods the body with bad fats and simple sugars. These are bad fuels and you cannot expect your mind to work without the correct fuel.

Even more important is the day of an exam. You need a really slow burning fuel for this day. Otherwise you risk running out of fuel halfway through the exam. You may not even recognise the symptoms - all you know is that this question is too difficult. No matter what you do you can't see how to do it.

But when you get home - and have something to eat - you realise how to do that same question!!

Now there are other possible explanations. But by eating a slow burning fuel - one that will last throughout the exam - you eliminate the possibility that lack of fuel caused you to fail! Try a cheese sandwich on wholemeal bread and a banana. Experiment with food until you have a perfect combination for exams.

TIP 92

I could never, ever study for hours at a time

Your body is not designed to sit still for long periods of time. Once you've completed a half hour's History revision, say, stand up and stretch. A few moments gentle stretching gets your blood circulating again and you return to your desk refreshed.

Remember that it is easier to deliver 100% effort on a small task rather than on a big one. And when you've finished the 4 half hour sessions, with your 5 minute breaks in between, come back to this tip and put a tick in the following box:

I *can* study for hours at a time. ☐

Tick here

TIP 93

Where do parents fit in?

Apart from keeping your brother and sister out of your room, you shouldn't expect anything else from your parents. Your home has to go on whether there is a student in the house or not. And having your meals prepared in a house with a roof over your head, for which you probably don't pay rent, is enough for anyone. Don't expect more. And if you get more from some considerate parent, be grateful.

TIP 94

How to get marks for questions you can't do

In Mathematics, marks are usually given for:

A clear diagram with all information on it	1 mark
Any relevant formulae	1 mark
Substitution into the formulae	1 mark
Correct answer	<u>1 mark</u>
	Total: 4 marks

Hence, by doing the first three, it may be possible to get 3 marks out of 4, that's 75%, without getting the answer!

You can modify this approach for all your subjects.

TIP 95

More on essay writing

Learn the facts! You must know *what* before you can ask *why*.

For example:

> Fact: During the Vietnam War, the Vietnamese dug underground tunnels.
>
> You must know this fact before you can ask:
>
>> Why did the Vietnamese dig tunnels?
>>
>> When did the Vietnamese start digging tunnels?
>>
>> Where did these tunnels lead? How long were they?
>>
>> How were they dug?
>>
>> Have other countries dug tunnels like these before? What similarities between them were there?
>>
>> If these tunnels had not been dug, what change in the war could have occurred?
>>
>> Are these tunnels still there today? Can a use be found for them now?

Also, consider a skeletal diagram. They help you organise your thoughts while you are making them up. And they are extremely easy to study from!

Heading	Subheadings	Details
	Who are they?	
Assyrians	When	
	Etc	

100 Study Tips that Work!

And lastly: In essay writing you may like to see if you have followed the following guidelines:

1. Be as informative as the question implies. But don't state everything you know. An exam question is not an opportunity for a memory dump. Just answer the question.

2. On the other hand, the examiner is not a mind reader. The examiner will mark what you have written - not what you know. So: *state what you know!*

3. Don't write what you believe to be false - state what you believe and justify your position. You are *not* asked to agree with the question. You *are* asked to justify any opinion you offer.

4. Don't offer your opinion unless necessary. If the question asks why Macbeth murdered Duncan, don't tell the examiner what you would have done.

5. Don't state any opinion - yours or someone else's, without giving evidence.

6. Only state relevant material. Otherwise you would find students demanding marks for writing down their telephone number. *"But it's correct! Why don't I get a mark?"*

7. Check that no statement is ambiguous. If you were to write that "Moses was the daughter of Pharaoh's son", it may be perfectly plain to you that Pharaoh had a daughter and she had a son called Moses. But that is not what you have written. Ambiguity should never be tolerated.

100 Study Tips that Work!

TIP 96

Movie directors went to school too

In reading a History text, think like a movie director. The book says "Ptolemy sailed to Egypt". Imagine you are writing a film script. You could make a complete blockbuster movie from this one sentence. Imagine the sorts of things you could do with this idea. Make the idea come to life and you'll enjoy the studying much more. Your marks will improve. You may even become the new Spielberg.

TIP 97

Different techniques for different subjects

Text books are necessary for Mathematics and Science. But for Business and Economics you can use textbooks only so much. Reading newspapers and watching the news are much more important for these subjects. Examiners expect you to take an interest in current affairs.

Textbooks are only part of language courses as well. You should read and write languages at any opportunity. Listen to tapes or current affairs in the language of choice. Subscribe to a pay TV channel in the language you are studying.

TIP 98

Tips for Maths Students

1. If you know that you have made a mistake in a problem, try to find it before you ask for help. Finding mistakes ranks highly among mathematicians as a skill.

2. Practise double checking : For instance, if you have just factorised an expression, remove the brackets to make sure you have not made a mistake.

3. Don't practise the hardest example you can find. Read the worked examples first and the easy worked examples first. The feeling that "I could do that!" is an excellent motivator to try one yourself - then to try a harder one yourself.

    You are not meant to reinvent Mathematics. Once you have mastered what has gone before, then you can try your hand at that too!

4. Check your answer - did the question ask for 2 decimal places, or 3 significant figures or scientific notation, or to the nearest dollar ? Have I calculated that the height of Mt Everest is 5cm?

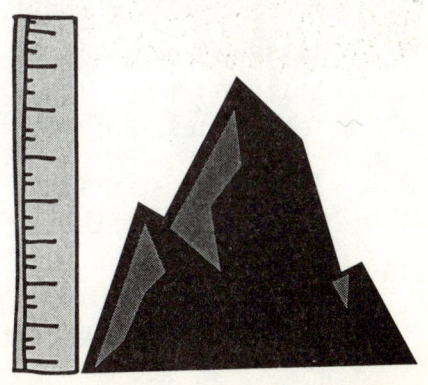

5   There are two Sins in Mathematics

    i)   Not fixing and recording mistakes in your Night-Before-Book

    ii)   Leaving a question blank in a test - *see Number 7 tip below.*

6   In Co-ordinate Geometry, the one question you never need to ask is: How do I draw this graph? You can always Plot Points to sketch any graph in the course.

7   You cannot answer the question: *Is it a hard exam question?* until you have

    i)   drawn a diagram - with all the information on it

    ii)   written down the formula(e)

    iii)   substituted into the formula(e)

Then perhaps you can tell.

Also, these three items would be the <u>best</u> Problem Solving Techniques. Use them and you are far more likely to figure out how to solve the problem completely.

8   It is very rare for you to be given a question that you can't score some marks for. Use the same techniques, diagram, formulae and substitution.

9   Do the questions that you find easy first - don't do Question 1, then Question 2 and so on. In that way, you will maximise your marks. Use your reading time - if they allow it - to choose the order in which you attempt the questions.

100 Study Tips that Work!

10   Don't waste time on calculations which seem to be getting nowhere. Marks are given for your diagram and formulae. Get these done and go on to the next question.

11   Some textbooks are good for theory, some are good for worked examples and some are good for exercises. Get several textbooks and become familiar with them.

12   You can find books that are designed for revision. They are ideal for the busy student. Find them.

13   Don't do complicated problems in your head. Write down the steps - neatly. Show the examiner each step that is needed. Use your calculator to evaluate where necessary.

14   Don't approximate the answers. Unless the question says to give your answer correct to 2 decimal places, say, then leave the answer unsimplified.

15   Some questions are given in parts. Question 4 may have part i) then part ii)

        4   i)   The area of a circle is $28.27u^2$. Show that its radius is $3u$

              ii)   Find the circumference of this circle

Let's say you can't do part i). Well, it's OK to use the value of the radius, $3u$, that they have given you in part i) in the second part of the question. Don't leave part ii) out if you can't do part i).

16   Diagrams should be large - about 1/3 of a page. Don't try to fit them on a postage stamp. If you are concerned about wasting paper, go and plant some trees. One tree will supply more paper than you can use in several lifetimes!

TIP 99

Twelve tips for exams

1. Get as many past papers as you can. Work through them trying to find areas of weakness in your preparation.

2. Prepare an Examination Revision Timetable. This should include the dates of each paper as well as your study times.

3. Some schools give open book exams, where you can bring in as many textbooks as you like. The point of these exams is to force you to be absolutely familiar with your textbook: so familiar that you can turn to the correct page and find the answer to any question. That's the way you should be for any type of exam - open book or not.

4. You can usually get some marks for any question. If you are running out of time in an essay exam, write a list of headings that could be used.

> **There is only one Iron clad Guarantee in exams. If you leave a question blank, you will get zero! Anything else may get you marks.**

100 Study Tips that Work!

5   Review your study techniques in the light of your exam results. Unless you consistently get 100%, your techniques may need changing.

6   Keep your watch on your desk. You cannot afford to go over time on any question.

7   Completing half an exam paper and getting what you did right, is better than doing all the paper and getting half wrong. With practice, you will get more and more correct. But if you continue to speed, you will continue to make careless errors.

8   Read each question intelligently, i.e. underline key words, work out which topic the question comes from, identify which type of question is being asked and jot down anything you think of on your answer page. Examiners will read jottings and award marks if they possibly can.

100 Study Tips that Work!

9   Make a decision as to whether to leave time at the end of your exam for checking. It may be worthwhile. But what if you don't finish the paper because you spent the time checking? This is a decision that you must make in the exam room.

10   Your work must be legible. This may mean that you have to change the way you write certain letters and numbers. If your 7's look like your y's, change one of them.

11   Look at how many marks each question is worth. If the first part of a question is worth 9 marks and the second part is worth 1 mark, then spend 9/10 of the time on part one and 1/10 of the time on part two. If you haven't been told how much each part is worth, use your judgement.

12   Your exam paper - with your teacher's corrections - is a most important document. Make sure you understand where you went wrong. Write up your mistakes and their corrections in your Night-Before-Book. Study them regularly!! Practise other questions of the same type.

TIP 100

The Last Word

By getting to the end of this book, you have shown that you have great determination.

You have shown that you can complete what you start.

And you will have left many others behind.

In completing it, you will have learned many things. But there is one *last* thing that you have shown about yourself.

Something that *was* always true. And *will* always be true.

Be aware of this one thing and your course will have been more than worthwhile. You will certainly improve your exam results even if you don't know it. But *unless* you know it, you will reach your limits very quickly.

What is this one last tip? It's this:

> *You are better than you think!*

> *In fact you are better than you can think!*

Realise this, understand this, treasure this and you can use the ideas in this book as a stepping stone to wherever you wish to go.

> Good luck with your studies.

> Vaya con Dios.

This book is available from any recognised bookseller or by contacting:

>Smith Mathematics
>
>14 Kooloona Crescent
>
>West Pymble   NSW   2073

Telephone :   (02) 9498 8883

Fax :   (02) 9498 4118

Other books available by the same author :

2 Unit Mathematics - HSC Practice Questions by Topic

3 Unit Mathematics - HSC Practice Questions by Topic

2 Unit Mathematics - 100 Mini HSC's

3 Unit Mathematics - 100 Mini HSC's

100 Mini Year 10 Exams - Mathematics Advanced Course
ideal for Years 10/11 Precalculus

Year 10 Mathematics - School Certificate Practice Exams